How T

MW01134482

An American Novelist Helps You Navigate The Maze

By Douglas Warren

© 2020

ISBN: 9781671418707

Cover photo: View from the 'top' of Menton near the border with Italy, on the French Riviera or Côte d'Azur. The land jutting out in the photo is Cap Martin, and just beyond lies Monaco.

Disclaimer: I am not a lawyer. This book is solely based on my personal experience.

Introduction

Have you thought of retiring somewhere exotic? Ever considered France? Or are you already a dyed-in-the-wool Francophile, taking every opportunity to visit France, studying its rich history, sampling the wonderful food and wine, and taking in the sights? Maybe you've even taken language courses? However, you won't really know the ins-and-outs of living in France until you actually do it full time. And that's not such a bad thing; in fact for this expat it has been quite an adventure. Hopefully I can help with your learning curve.

2

When I retired from my job in New York City and decided to travel to Paris I wasn't sure I'd stay. I really didn't know what I was getting into. Luckily in the nearly seven years I've been in Europe, mostly in France, it's gone very well, in fact much better than I dreamed. But don't get me wrong; there have been a few bumps in the road. Now, in retrospect, they've mostly been minor challenges.

Hopefully my story will help you fulfill your own dream. All of my insights and suggestions are just that: my personal opinions. To obtain my first visitor's visa I employed the services of a lawyer, which I highly recommend.

When I left for Paris without a visa I knew I could legally, armed with my recently renewed passport, stay in France for up to 90 days at a time. I also knew there were options for leaving France while still remaining in Europe or thereabouts. One option, for example, is to visit nearby North African countries. I spent 90 days in Morocco, an adventure in itself.

For the process of obtaining my first visitor's visa for France and its subsequent renewals I made a list based on my lawyer's recommendations, but also used the list provided on the website of the French Consulate in the States.

A word of caution: don't slavishly duplicate my lists. And this is important, the French government has an uncanny way of adding items and/or asking for information you weren't prepared to give. They sometimes, though not often, add items without stating such.

I think the French government likes tall stacks of papers. I did provide those sizable stacks. In other words, I provided more than they asked for. But let me give you a quick example of something that took me by surprise when I first went to renew my visa. I got divorced more than twenty years ago. When I went into the Paris Police Prefecture to renew my visa and obtain a French I.D. card (Titre de Sejour) the nice clerk wanted to know my ex-wife's date of birth as well as the date we were married. Luckily I didn't have to provide proof of those dates, but it did tax my memory. As I tried to recall the dates, the clerk smiled, amused by my obvious effort. We even shared a chuckle, despite the tense situation and language difference. I do know a little bit of the language, what I call caveman-French.

But I'm getting ahead of myself. Paperwork-wise the French government does not make it easy or simple to obtain a visa. They want to know many details. Provided you do your homework, and with the help of a lawyer, it is possible and relatively painless. Remember to do a lot of checking and re-checking to make sure you have everything in order.

If you speak, read and/or write French that's a big help. Like I mentioned, I don't. Instead I have relied on my friendly 'bonjour' greeting, and charming smile in dealing with government officials. I also used a good deal of pointing and bits of mime. While I can't prove this, I think being a senior citizen on my own helped, if only a little.

France by-far is the most visited country in the world, with the U.S. running a not-very-close second. France relies economically on this yearly influx of tourists. Being such, lots of French people, especially in Paris, speak a smattering of other languages, with English being the most widely known. But this isn't usually true in government offices. Bring a translator if you don't speak French. It will avoid confusion and help the process go much smoother. Silly me didn't do this for the first renewal appointment, so my anxiety level was off the charts. Still I did manage. I learned my lesson though and brought along an interpreter the second time I renewed. It also makes it easier for the prefecture clerk.

Chapter One – Why France?

Occasionally I meet Americans on vacation. (The majority of them are from New York City for some reason.) When they find out I live here full time they ask, 'why Paris?' Forgive me for this, but my usual smug reply is, 'because it's Paris.' I try to leave it at that, hoping they won't ask for details, hoping my obvious answer will suffice. But they always ask more questions. My guess is that they are longing to move here. They're seeking reassurance that it is possible and not as difficult or expensive as they've heard. This little book is my effort to answer some of those questions and give the reader a better idea of the process.

I love France and Paris in particular (who wouldn't?), for the food, wine, history, architecture, the art, the culture, and the old-worldly-ness. I love the music of the French language and hope to understand and speak more soon. While I can read some French, my attempts at pronouncing even simple French words puts a questioning look on most French faces. In fact sometimes they snicker, then quickly apologize. Regardless, I do try.

I think the feeling is mutual, that generally the French people like Americans and anything (other than the politics) that is American. Really, I've never met anyone in France who shunned me because of my nationality. I see many young people wearing New York Yankee baseball hats.

It's important to point out that lots of people in Paris (and some of the other larger cities), especially the young, speak some English, certainly much better than I speak French. That said; they do appreciate my attempts to speak a little bit of French, but then they quickly speak English in return. They want to practice their English. The music (Muzak) playing in stores is usually in English, mostly American. The same is true for American movies, very popular. The French can't help but pick up some English along the way.

Historically America has very strong ties to France. Depending on how you read history, there's ample evidence that the Marquis de Lafayette and the French Navy (with the support of the king of course) were the absolute deciding factors in the American Revolution. I'll stop there with the history lesson.

Chapter Two – Where to live

I'm guessing, but when most Americans think of France they automatically think of Paris, followed closely by the Riviera, particularly Cannes with its film festival. Those are the biggies. Maybe other Riviera towns also come to mind, like Nice and possibly Saint-Tropez, Antibes, and even Marseille. There's also Monaco, separate from France, while being surrounded by it. Lesser known would be Toulon with its large naval base, and Montpellier with its university, and possibly Menton near the border with Italy, as shown on the cover of this book.

But there's a host of other towns, cities, and villages throughout France just waiting to be explored. Though often overlooked there's also the island of Corsica, the birthplace of Napoleon I. I don't intend to turn this chapter into a travelogue, as there are so many who have done expertly detailed explorations of France. I simply intend to provide a glimpse into my own travels. Admittedly I am interested in French history and that has influenced my travels. Perhaps you have a special interest? It could be anything or a long list of interests, such as architecture, religion, fishing, wine, cheese, geography, sports, education, language. The options seem endless.

Mostly I've stayed in the places I'll mention for one month. In a few for several months. Once I lived in Paris uninterrupted for two years. In traveling and living in different places it was always with an eye toward settling down and making it my permanent residence in France.

After nearly seven years of roaming around France and Europe, and even three months in Morocco, I've finally found a village where I intend to stay. It's called Alet-les-Bains, located about a half hour drive south of Carcassonne, which is a fascinating small city in itself, with a magnificent citadel. Centuries ago Carcassonne was on the border between France and Spain. So the entire area has been influenced by Spain, particularly by the region of Catalonia. More about Alet-les-

Bains later. First, I'll provide a brief sketch of the places I've lived for a month or more as well as those I've visited.

The first is Paris. Along with New York City, my most favorite of cities. In fact, it's worthwhile comparing the two a little. New York, where I lived for about ten years, is definitely the financial center of the US and also has considerable political and cultural clout as well. It's one of the oldest cities in America, dripping with history going back to when it was called New Amsterdam. Even then it was a center of commerce and rather than being settled for religious reasons like early Boston, from the beginning NYC has been a party town. But unlike the center of Paris, NYC (as in Manhattan) is constantly changing and rebuilding, as in the line from that song, 'the city that never sleeps.'

By contrast, Paris proper is a museum-piece. Sort of an adult's Disneyland, a good mockup of itself on the outside, while inside always modernizing. To clarify, walking through Paris you see those marvelous Haussmann apartment buildings with their balconies and mansard roofs. He did a wonderful job of sculpting the modern boulevards and buildings of Paris. But did the soul of Paris get destroyed in the process? I wonder. From what I've read about pre-Haussmann Paris it was a disguising dirty town full of twisty narrow streets, open sewers, and garbage everywhere. Haussmann did much urban-renewal, establishing those wide boulevards and many beautiful parks. However, some areas of Paris were just too challenging for him. Luckily for modern Paris lovers like myself there are still a few of those narrow winding streets and ancient buildings left to discover. This is particularly true on butte Montmartre.

If you get the chance to look inside, the apartments in are as modern as any in Manhattan. To extend the analogy of Disneyland, Paris is 'authentic' on the outside, but that's only a façade.

There's one notable exception to the elegance of Paris proper, the Montparnasse Tower. I don't like the building, if for no other reason because it doesn't fit in at all with the rest of the city. It belongs in lower Manhattan or the business section of Paris just outside of the city, an area called La Défense. That's where all the high-rise office towers are located. How the Montparnasse Tower got built I'll never know. There may have been some political finagling involved.

Naturally, both cities are very expensive! If you want to live in either Paris proper, or Manhattan, you'll have to spend many millions. Outside of Paris the costs go down, but then you aren't in Paris anymore. You'll be spending much time on trams or the Metro or RER trains getting into and back out of the city. And all are crowded, even during the virus crisis.

The same is true for NYC. The prices for rent continue to increase. I can't afford to live in Paris or New York anymore. That said, I did spend many good years in both cities, enjoying the sights and history. Unfortunately, this past year, due to the train strike and virus, it was no longer enjoyable living in or around Paris. That's why I've moved to a country village in the mountains.

The second French city I lived in, and France's second city, is Marseille. As many warned me, 'don't go to Marseille, it's a dangerous place full of gangsters and drug dealers.' Evidently lots of people were impressed by the movie, The French Connection.

Although Marseille is a little gritty in parts, it is mostly a beautiful Mediterranean city. This is especially true along the old waterfront where there are elegant apartment buildings and wonderful restaurants looking out on waters filled with luxury yachts. Marseille has splendid museums, and being on the sea there's plenty of watersports as well as basking in the sun. You might even consider Marseille glamorous. Another bonus in that area is Aix-en-Provence, just a short train ride away from Marseille. But beware, you'll probably hear more English spoken there than French! Bring lots of Euros for exploring the upscale boutiques. Even Apple has a store there. One fact about Marseille that surprised me, the city is older than Paris, first established as a Greek colony.

Further down the coast toward Spain is the small city of Narbonne where the Midi Canal terminates into the Mediterranean. The canal crosses the whole of France, beginning at the Bay of Biscay on the Atlantic side. It's an ancient canal, now mostly used by pleasure boats. Narbonne is a beautiful old city with one of the few bridges left in Europe that actually has shops on the bridge. If not living where I am now, Narbonne would be high on my list of alternatives, there and Menton. That might be a hard decision for you, deciding where to live, as there are so many wonderful options throughout France. But if Paris is your dream town, as it was mine, then go for it!

That said, let me give you a few more options. I spent five months in Perpignan, also in the south and close to, but not on the coast. I was warned not to go there during the winter because of the wind, but I went anyway. Silly me. What a terribly windy place. Not as bad as Chicago, but pretty darn bad. I'm no weatherman, however I speculate that Perpignan acts as a wind tunnel between the mountains and the sea.

The town does have some redeemable features though, like a surprisingly impressive art museum featuring artists from the area. Salvador Dali declared Perpignan the center of the universe.

There's also a formidable citadel, certainly not as spectacular as the one in Carcassonne, but impressive just the same. It was built by a local king who shortly thereafter got run out of town by a rival king. The town also boasts a remarkable gatehouse with a museum inside. The gatehouse also contains a tower that you can climb up. There's a narrow circular balcony on top that provides a panoramic view of the city and the snow-covered mountains in the distance. Despite my vertigo, I braved the climb up to that little balcony, all the while holding on to the railing for dear life. I found the old town the most fascinating part of the city with its old apartment buildings and narrow streets.

In the north of France, just across the Channel from England, is Boulogne-sur-Mer. It's a few kilometers south of Calais, near enough to the Channel tunnel and ferry to jump over to the UK should the urge strike you to try some English food and have a chat in your own language.

 Unfortunately, during WWII the waterfront of Boulogne-sur-Mer was heavily bombed, so that part of the city had to be rebuilt after the war. There is now a very nifty aquarium along the waterfront.

Geographically the hills of the town rise quickly on both sides of the bay, topped on one side by the old walled village, still occupied by a few dozen medieval houses and an impressive cathedral. But the weather's not so much different from England, with lots of fog and rain. This was the only city on the Channel and Bay of Biscay I visited. Admittedly I'm partial to warm weather and the Mediterranean.

The Paris suburb of Champigny-sur-Marne I enjoyed the most of the many Paris suburbs where I've stayed. It was a joy to spend three months close to the river Marne, where there is a tree-lined riverside park on both banks of the river. I lived on the edge of Champigny-sur-Marne where it meets Joinville-le-Pont. Just outside the apartment is a bridge across the Marne and another bridge in Joinville-le-Pont, so I could cross the nearest bridge and walk along the far bank then cross back over the other bridge for the walk home. In Joinville-le-Pont there is an old but still used water tunnel that provides a shortcut to the Seine. Near the entrance to the tunnel many riverboats are anchored.

There are several riverside restaurants in that area as well. Despite the restrictions of the virus I enjoyed a very pleasant summer there in 2020.

Now a few words about my new home, Alet-les-Bain. That's its official name, but the locals simply call it Alet, pronouncing the 't' as in Alette. I live on one of the main streets, actually more like trails, where there's barely enough room for one car to pass through and no parking allowed. On the edge of the village are places to park making it necessary for the villagers to walk to their houses. Luckily the village is small, and the walk is short. It's very popular among tourists who pay a small fee to walk through the ruins of the abbey, then walk the streets to photograph the medieval houses. An extra bonus is the mineral springs first discovered by the Romans. During the summer months a large swimming pool is filled with the supposedly healing spring water. Even with the near constant tourist traffic the village is quiet and peaceful, perfect for writing.

The village boosts three hotels:

- Hostellerie de l'Evêché with a full service restaurant, located in a riverside park.

- Les Marguerites B&B with beautiful gardens. Les Marguerites holds special events like ethnic-themed dinners, movies, and quiz nights. It's run by an English couple and their family.

- The third hotel is located on the main street and adjacent to the Val D'Aleth campground along the river.

There's one a small grocery shop called Annie's, located across from the ruins of the Abbey. During the season Annie's features a terrace with tables to sit and have a coffee or snack. Also during the season a company next to the river offers white-water rafting and canoe rentals.

The storefront where one enters the ruins also serves as the tourist information office and post office. It's a historical village dating back to Roman times. At the moment there are a few houses for sale. Whether you are just passing through or fall in love with Alet-les-Bains as I have, it's well worth a look. Just up the road from the village is a casino, though not on the scale of Monte Carlo, it does offer food and entertainment for gamblers.

That's the thumbnail sketch of my travels. After you've become well acquainted with Paris and its surrounds I suggest you tour the palaces of Versailles and Fontainebleau and take the train down to explore the Medieval village of Provins with its surrounding battlements and the tower built on a hill in the center of town. There's a splendid little museum by the tower. The village is about an hour and a half outside of Paris. An often-missed sight near Paris is the basilica St. Denis. It's the first church built in the Gothic style and the final resting place for French kings and queens.

Chapter Three – Preparing

In 2012 I left my job in Manhattan. I took an early retirement at 62. It was time. I spent the next year deciding what to do with myself. Should I start living my dream of becoming a writer in Paris? The whole idea seemed pretty scary and overwhelming, but also exciting. When I told my friends my plan they thought I was nuts. Perhaps I was a little, but now they're envious.

A couple of years before retiring I visited my son who lives in London, followed by a week in Paris. I fell in love with Paris all over again. You see, long ago as a teenager I spent three months in Europe. I dreamed of living in Paris. However, life took me in other directions and slowly the dream faded into the background, but it never completely disappeared. After that trip to see my son I again began dreaming of living in Paris as well as traveling and writing. But how to go about such a radical change, moving to a different country where I spoke very little of the language? Where to start?

I did my research mostly online. I learned about the Schengen Agreement, of only being allowed to stay in certain European countries, mostly members of the EU, for a maximum of 90 days at a time. In the Schengen rule, with an American passport, you must leave **all of the Schengen Agreement countries** after 90 days and stay out for 90 days. Then you can return for another 90 days. I thought moving around like that would be a good way to figure out if I really wanted to permanently live in France or perhaps elsewhere in Europe. I kept an open mind about that for a long time. As it turned out the next four years of traveling in and around Europe were very interesting and agreeable. Everywhere I went people were friendly and helpful even if they didn't speak much English. But we all got by. (Like a friend keeps reminding me, a fistful of Euros can help communications immensely.)

14

Caution: Well-meaning but misinformed people will tell you that all you have to do is leave France for a few hours, then the 90-day clock is reset. This was true at one time, but no longer applies. It probably dates back to the days before the EU was formed. Those well-meaning people are wrong. This was also true about marrying a local; you were automatically allowed to stay if you married a French citizen. However, the whole marriage situation has gotten much more complicated and varies from country to country, even within the EU. If you happen to fall in love and naturally want to stay, you'd better discuss your residency options with an immigration lawyer. True, there are ways to stay in France if you get married, but it isn't an automatic process. Better talk to an expert.

One of the convenient exceptions to the 90-day rule is the UK, which is not part of the Schengen Agreement. There you can stay for up to 6 months solely based on your U.S. passport. But if you are set on retiring to France you'll probably want to return there after 90 days. Of course all or some of these rules may change because of Brexit. Also, The Republic of Ireland didn't sign the Schengen Agreement, so you can stay in France for 90 days without a visa, hop over to Ireland for 90 days then go back to France for another 90 days. I did that twice and it worked out fine. It is impossible to leave out mention of the virus and the air travel situation. After all you can't retire in France if you can't get over here.

Here's one example of the current situation. My son and his wife visited me in Paris in January of 2020. They were determined to go back to Los Angeles where they live and get visas. They did acquire their visas but couldn't come back to Paris because of the travel restrictions. They haven't found out if they need to reapply for their visas once the travel restrictions are lifted. Certainly they aren't the only ones in that predicament, on both sides of the Atlantic.

When I decided to leave New York to spend my first 90 days in Paris I found a reasonably priced studio apartment in the Belleville section of Paris through Craigslist. I needed to watch my expenses, since at the time I was living solely on my pension and savings. That was in 2013 and I certainly didn't trust Craigslist even back then. But I didn't know about airbnb and other alternatives. Later my son in London, told me about airbnb, since he often travels for work. Having studied in France he speaks the language and was nice enough to take the Eurostar train to Paris to check out the apartment. This was while I was still in New York. If he felt the place was acceptable and the landlord reasonable I authorized him to leave a deposit. I wired the money and he secured the apartment for me. He did a fine job in a very short time. He accomplished all that in one day, taking an early train, checking out the apartment, leaving the deposit, then took a late train back to London.

Belleville, a former village just outside of Paris, now lies within the 20th Arrondissement. It's known for its history of radicalism. Today there are still elements of left-leaning groups and a smattering of artist studios. Students and hipsters enjoy Belleville's nightlife, although some have moved on to the Bastille section of Paris. Evidently being hip in Paris is 'a moveable feast.' (Belleville is still my favorite Paris neighborhood.)

That was it; I had a place to live in Paris. Next, I got rid of everything in my Hell's Kitchen apartment, packed a suitcase (all my worldly possessions), took the subway out to JFK Airport and the next morning I was in Paris beginning my new life.

That's my story about leaving New York. If it sounds a bit hasty, remember it took place over a six-month period before I actually got on the plane. It gave me plenty of time to get rid of everything in my apartment as well as time to change my mind. Most importantly, it gave me time to prepare to live in France, including research on French culture and customs. After all, who wants to stick out like a tourist?

Chapter Four – Selecting a Lawyer

Even if you speak fluent French and think you can manage to get a visa on your own, do yourself a favor and *don't*. It's just too complicated a process. Also, don't listen to well-meaning advice from friends, family, and especially the Internet. There's a lot of bogus websites that claim to help you sort out the visa process. Well maybe it worked for that person, but do you really want to trust someone *you don't know and didn't pay* to advise you on such an important matter?

As stated, I hired a lawyer and it was well worth the expense. While not a guarantee that I would be granted a visitors visa, it certainly helped to use an expert. I talked to four different immigration lawyers before deciding. Here's why I didn't choose three of those lawyers and felt confident with my ultimate choice:

1. One lawyer, although advertising to be an immigration specialist, wasn't able to answer some basic questions.

2. Another lawyer seemed too busy to just sit down and have a chat with me. In other words, not seeing the potential for making a considerable amount of money, gave me the brush-off without offering to referring me to another lawyer.

3. The third lawyer knew very little English, making it very difficult to communicate and understand instructions.

The lawyer I finally decided on is an American who speaks fluent French and specializes in immigration issues. Because he was willing to sit down and talk to me for over an hour to decide if it was a 'good fit,' that's what convinced me.

Incidentally, having my paperwork typed on the lawyer's letterhead I believed helped my case. Not that the person at the consulate was intimidated by my use of a lawyer, but it did seem to carry some weight. For instance, and this turned out to be a big issue, the lady at the consulate demanded that I present a copy of the I.D. card of my landlord in Paris. Since I had a lease I insisted that my lawyer informed me I didn't need my landlord's I.D. The lady at the consulate finally backed down. Now I'm not saying you should challenge the French consulate (or its proxy) on any point, as it's possible your application will be rejected (because they can). It's best to have all your ducks in a row to avoid any sort of trouble.

Chapter Five – The Visa Application Process

After over four years of travel I finally decided France, and primarily Paris, was the place for me. It was time to apply for a year-long, but renewable, visitor's visa. France, like many European countries, has a complex (and some say convoluted) visa application process; luckily less so for a visitor's visa. I don't say that to belittle these countries, on the contrary the world is a very complicated place and immigration policies are necessary. Therefore, it's best to seek help from an experienced immigration lawyer. The more I researched, (mostly online) about getting a visitor's visa, the more I realized I needed professional help. There's a lot of good basic information on the Internet about retiring and moving to France and other countries, but the more I looked the more the information of one website contradicted what I read on other sites. The visa landscape is forever changing. Also, some of those websites are old. Rules, regulations, and costs have changed.

It's best to invest in the help of a lawyer whose job it is to keep well-informed. (Mine unfortunately wasn't as informed or informative as I had hoped and expected.) The cost for using a lawyer usually runs between $1500-2500 depending on the complexity of your situation. For a single person like myself, on a pension, seeking a visitor's visa, the process is fairly straightforward. For a couple it will be more complicated. You will have to document your income and have enough in the bank to live on without working. Not to say you have to be wealthy, as the basic income requirement is equal to the French minimum wage. It is required that you have proof of income such as a letter from Social Security. A registered French translator must translate both the letter and your birth certificate into French. Translations *must be dated less than three months* from your visa appointment. I paid about € 50 each for the translations.

I am writing about *retiring* in France. Know that if you're planning to work or start a business the process is much more complicated and requires more paperwork as well as different types of visas. Therefore, it will be more expensive and more important to use a lawyer. I had an income from my pension and savings and had no plans to work or study. In other words, I was self-sufficient and therefore would not be a financial burden on the French government. Obviously in a small way the French economy benefits from my financial independence.

Income Requirements: If you are retired and receiving income through investments, savings, and a pension (including Social Security) you'll have to *prove* your income meets the required minimum. That income amount currently stands at roughly € 1,500 per month. You'll have to sign a statement verifying that *you will not work* in France. Your lawyer should supply this statement in French. All you'll have to do is sign it. A letter is also required stating *why* you want to live in France. This can be a single page letter. Only you can answer the question, try to be specific. Your lawyer should help you with this letter and might even provide examples.

For your first year you'll have to prove you have private health insurance. And that you have a doctor. It's best to bring a letter from your French doctor simply stating that you are under his or her care. There are a few doctors listed on the American embassy website, but some are quite pricy.

In short, the French government wants plenty of proof you will not be a financial burden during your year-long stay. My lawyer recommended a health insurance company. The cost for a year was about $900. For the second year and henceforth, since you'll have been residing in France for more than three months, you'll be eligible for the French national health plan and will be issues the insurance card called the Carte Vitale, along with a Social Security number. The card can be obtained at the local CPAM office. The initials stand for

Caisse Primaire d'Assurances Maladie, the local department level of the national health insurance administration. The SS number will only be used by the national health service, unless you become employed.

Finally, you'll need to prove you have a place to live in France. This can be tricky if you are currently living in the U.S. and haven't arranged for housing in France. Even though I found a long-term place to stay in Paris through airbnb, my host (landlord) and I came to an agreement and we signed a one-year lease for the same time period as my visa. But I was already in Paris, so it was easy to make that arrangement.

You'll have to prove you have a place to live, whether in a hotel or renting an apartment or a room in an apartment. This must all be completed before you apply for your visa. There are housing services that will help you find accommodations and provide the necessary paperwork. But a word of caution: there are many scammers out there.

Before beginning the process of obtaining a visa I'd read online that one must return to one's home in the U.S. to apply for a visa. You can't apply while you're in France, you *must* return to the U.S. That was the first question I asked my lawyer in Paris. I didn't want to hear about that requirement, as I had no desire to make the trip to California and back solely to apply for the visa. I'd given up my apartment in New York and changed my address of record to my other son's home in Los Angeles. However, much to my chagrin, I did have to make the trip to apply for the visa at the French Consulate in L.A.

Note: Recently I visited the French Consulate's website in Los Angeles. To my surprise the consulate no longer processes visa applications. The French government has contracted with a private company to process visa applications. It's hard to say how this relationship will work out, so it's best to check with the nearest consulate to see if this still applies.

Here's what the consulate's website stated:

"The visa section of the consulate general of France in Los Angeles has ceased operation on 06/27/2018. All application will be processed by:

VFS Global
Century City, 1901 Avenue of the Stars
Regus Centre - 2nd Floor
Los Angeles CA 90067

There are 9 VFS Centers in the US: Atlanta, Boston, Chicago, Houston, Los Angeles, Miami, New York, San Francisco, and Washington. Visa seekers can apply at the VFS Center of their choice.

Appointments with VFS can be booked through the French visa website. On this website you will also find all the information you need to gather the required documentation."

Even though VFS Global will be handling the visa applications it is likely the visa requirements will, for the most part, remain the same.

French Consulate in Los Angeles

As mentioned, at the time I applied the French Consulate was still processing visas. Briefly here's my experience traveling from Paris to L.A. and back. Since my address of record is no longer New York City but Los Angeles, I *had* to go to the French Consulate office in L.A. to start my visa application process. At that point I'd been living in Europe for four years and had no desire to return to the States. That is to say, I felt at home over here. There were several reasons for not wanting to return, not the least of which: the political chaos. Plus, I like living in Europe. Other reasons included not wanting to fly from Paris to L.A. and back. (I hate to fly, not because of the actually flying, but because of the security checks, horribly cramped quarters, the delays, and the waiting.) Plus, there's the expense of travel, and finding a place to live in L.A. for a month. However, since I am retired the overriding reason for not going to the States was the cost. There were a few problems I had to work through, but the trip was successful, and I did get to spend some time with my son and his wife.

Chapter Six – Life as an Expat

In the four years prior to applying for a French visa I was doing what I call *The-Schengen-Shuffle*. To leave the Schengen area for three months at a time I visited England twice, Ireland twice, Morocco once, and Albania twice. (It was in Martil, Morocco, after being in Europe for a year, that I began to write my first novel.)

In the UK, with an American passport, you can visit for up to 6 months at a time. I took advantage of this long stay once, no problem. Although on my next trip to the UK from Paris via the Eurostar, I was pulled aside by UK security while still in Paris and questioned about how long I had been away from the United States. After answering their questions they did allow me to board the train. However, they stated that in order to enter the UK in the future I would have to return to the US, as I had been in Europe for over two years. Luckily I kept my mouth shut, not protesting what I saw as an arbitrary ruling by the UK border patrol. (I've never read anything anywhere about having to periodically return to the US.) To their credit the security officers were very kind and even helped me with my luggage.

If you aren't quite ready to become a permanent resident in France, I suggest you do as I did. It's much cheaper as well. Buy a round trip ticket to Paris and book the return flight within that 90-day window. You can use the return ticket to come back to the States and sort out your life in preparation for a longer stay in France. If you are absolutely certain you want to stay in Europe, do as I did: throw away that return ticket and commit to becoming an expat.

Still, I wasn't sure I wanted to stay in Paris permanently and start the process of obtaining a visa. I knew it would be a long and arduous process, not to mention the expense. I took my time and every 90 days I left and explored other parts of Europe. My first trip out of France after my initial three-month stay was to the UK, which is outside the

24

Schengen territory. While the Republic of Ireland is part of the EU, it didn't sign the Schengen Agreement. I stayed there for 90 days on two separate occasions.

Staying in Ireland or the UK is quite expensive, more so than on the continent. Always conscious of keeping within my retirement budget I started looking for inexpensive places to spend my 90 days out of the Schengen area. In my research I discovered that Albania is quite affordable, both in rent and living expenses. It's situated north of Greece and less than 72 km (45 miles) from Italy across the Strait of Otranto. The coast of Albania touches the Adriatic Sea to the west and the Ionian Sea to the southwest, forming what is called the 'Albanian Riviera.'

Since I was going in that direction from where I was staying in Menton, France (see cover photo) I decided to spend a month in Rome before taking the train across Italy to Bari, then the ferry across to Albania. The ferry was a relaxing overnight trip and after a short bus ride from the Albanian port of Durrës I was in Tirana, the capital.

Eventually I found out that because of the large number of Peace Corp workers in Albania any American can live there for up to a year without a visa. If I really liked it I could extend my stay, thus saving a lot of money. But it didn't work out that way, after all Tirana is no Paris and Albania, though rich in history, can't compare to the culture and architecture of France. In fact, Albania's poverty reminded me of Morocco, being nearly a third-world country. Still, if you want to save some money you might consider Albania since it is centrally located. If you have a car you can explore Greece and other surrounding countries. At this writing, although Albania has railroad tracks, it doesn't have a train system. While some of the young people in Tirana speak English, most Albanians don't. The Albanian language is extremely difficult to learn, since it isn't directly related to any other language or language group. By contrast, the French use many English words and phrases and vice versa.

Back in Paris

This is very important: When you arrive in Paris after getting your visa (the initial part), make sure you get your passport stamped at the airport. Explain your situation to the agent *before* handing over your passport. I didn't and they did a haphazard job of stamping my passport, making it nearly illegible. If you ask politely they *might* make an extra effort to do a good job with the stamp.

Once you arrive in France there are two more steps involved in finalizing your visa. The first is the medical exam, the second is a final interview where all of your paperwork is reviewed, and you will have to pay the € 250 stamp tax. (This can now be done online and must be done before the final interview).[1]

In order to get these appointments you first have to supply a copy of your completed visa application, a copy of the photo page of your passport, a copy of your visa that was pasted into your passport, plus, as mentioned, a copy of the entry stamp from when you arrived in France. The visa application instructions *suggest* that you mail those documents to the OFII office nearest you. (Office Français de l'Immigration et de l'Intégration). For me this turned out to be a big mistake, mailing those documents, for the envelope either never made it to the OFII office, or once received was somehow misplace. That's a lot of important documents to go missing!

After mailing those copies I waited 2-1/2 months for notification of my appointments. It was a long nail-biting wait. Finally, in desperation, I took copies of everything to the OFII office. There the front desk lady

---

[1] https://www.timbresofii.fr/pages/choixTimbres.jsp

stamped the date on the application and told me it would take about a month to receive my appointment time. Within a week I got a confirmation of receipt of my documents, but I did have to wait about a month to receive the actual appointment time, first via e-mail, followed by a confirmation letter. I'll never know what happened to that envelope with all my vital information. The moral of the story: don't mail your documents, hand deliver them and make sure the person who receives the envelope stamps the date received in your presence.

The Medical Examination

Because I live in Paris the appointment for my medical exam was at the Paris area OFII medical office located in Montrouge, a southern suburb of Paris.

For my 8:30 AM appointment I arrived early, about 7:45. Since at the time I lived in the 18th arrondissement and the appointment was on the other side of Paris, I took the M4 Metro line to the Montparnasse station and transferred to the M13. That got me within a few blocks of the OFII office. It took about an hour to get there, door-to-door. I was one of the first in line. The doors opened at 8:00. Those with 8:00 appointments were admitted first. At about 8:15 I, along with 8 others, was admitted, with each of us checking in at reception where they examine your appointment letter. Then we were directed into a waiting room. About 45 minutes later we were ushered into the actual medical waiting area. This large room is divided into separate areas, what I call stations, for each step of the process: the receptionist questions; the general medical exam, including an eye test, weight and height, and a blood-sugar test; the x-ray station; and lastly meeting with the doctor who reviews the results.

I waited until the receptionist called my name. Keep alert for your name being called. You might not recognize your own name with a

French accent. Since I was first in line they called me first. The entire exam process is efficient and the staff very friendly and helpful. After a few general health questions the receptionist explained that I should sit with my paperwork in the next waiting area where a technician would call me by name.

Luckily the receptionist, who was first to interview me, and the doctor who was last to interview me, both spoke passable English. The technician knew limited English but was friendly and efficient. The process only took a few minutes, then I was escorted to a booth and instructed to remove my shirt for the chest x-ray. The booth had a locking door, with a door opposite that the x-ray technician soon opened and took me into the x-ray room. A minute later I was back in the little booth putting my shirt on. I then went to the next waiting area for the final medical exam by a doctor. After just a minute or two the doctor came out and escorted me to another private booth with a locking door. Again I was instructed to take off my shirt. But as I sat in the doctor's office where my test results were explained I wondered why I had to sit there bare-chested. That was never explained, and I didn't ask. I passed all of the tests. The doctor gave me two copies of a document that she stamped and signed and told me to take the documents to my final interview at the Bastille neighborhood office. True there was a 45-minute wait beforehand, but the actual physical exam process took less than half an hour.

At the Bastille immigration office I presented the receipt for the fee (tax stamp) that I'd paid online, and the second portion of the visa was added to my passport. That was it. I was done, home-free for an entire year in France.

In Conclusion

As I have mentioned, obtaining a visa can seem an overwhelming process. My advice is to take it a little at a time, use the services of a lawyer, and with patience you'll get your visitors visa. Two important things you will need in order to *renew* your visa are a French phone number to receive important text messages, and a French bank account. Certainly a phone is easy to get. However, due to new U.S. banking laws it will be difficult to get a French bank account. The post office bank won't give an account to an American and neither will some regular banks. If you can't find a bank willing to give you an account then you'll have to go to the Bank of France. The national bank will assign a bank to give you an account. Armed with a letter from the national bank, the bank they assign you will be required to give you an account.

Whether you plan to do some 'test living' in France, or have decided to get the visa, you'll soon be enjoying the wonder that is France.

A Brief Update – August 2019

Recently, on the 16th of August, I went for my appointment (rendez-vous) at the Police Prefecture in Paris to renew my visitor's visa. This office, located on The Île de la Cité, is where those living in Paris must go to renew their visa. I made the appointment online back in March. You can only make an appointment less than six moths from the date that your visa expires. You are given a choice of three or four days and times.

Luckily and by accident the appointment I choose turned out to be perfect in two ways. First, it was a Friday afternoon and second, and most importantly, it was the day after a national holiday. Because of these two factors the waiting room was practically empty. It was only a few minutes wait.

Even though you will have a specific time for your appointment it is very likely that the staff will fall behind in the appointments and you might have a long wait, as I did the first year I renewed. That first year appointment came right before lunch, so I had to wait an extra hour for the staff to return from lunch.

This time I took an interpreter since my grasp of the French language is still minimal. Having the interpreter made the appointment much easier than last year when I went alone.

The only snag in the entire process was the health insurance paperwork. I did obtain a national health card (Carte Vitale) and had it with me. However, the card doesn't show its expiration date. Luckily the oldest hospital in Paris, Hôtel-Dieu de Paris, is just across the street, so my interpreter and I went over to the hospital pharmacy where they kindly printed out the information I was missing. We then went back to the Prefecture and completed the process.

I just needed to receive that all-important text from the Prefecture giving me a date and time to pick up my new visa. I did get the text and went in with my tax payment receipt for €269 and current visa and was given my new visa. Hurray! Good for another year.

Another Brief Update – September 2020

As I mentioned in the new chapter on where to live in France, I recently moved to the south of France again. On the 1st of September I packed up and took the train from Gare de Lyon in Paris to Carcassonne, then a bus to Alet-les-Bain, a small medieval village. A week later I was back in Carcassonne attempting to renew my visa. Wisely I had hired an interpreter ahead of time to smooth the interview. Since Carcassonne is a small city, compared to Paris, it was a painless process and we were in and out in only half an hour. Of course this was my third renewal, so I had all the kinks worked out in the years prior. Because my appointment was in the morning I didn't want to take the chance of being held up by a late bus, so I arrived the night before and stayed at the reasonably decent and affordable Hotel Le Central, literally around the corner from the prefecture office. Now I just have to wait for that all-important text giving me an appointment time to come and get my new visa. They said it would be a few months, but then I have a temporary visa to carry. It's good until March of 2021.

That's something to consider in applying for your visa, if it's in Paris it will take longer and is more complicated, whereas the process is faster and easier in a smaller city. As a footnote to all of this, when I renewed my passport I went through the consulate office in Marseille since I was living in Perpignan at the time. I was shocked to receive my new passport one week from the day I sent the old one to Marseille. Sometimes smaller is better!

Appendices

Below are lists of essential documents and/or actions you will need to take in obtaining a visitor's visa. Also included is a list of items you will need to renew your visa.

Appendix I

The essential checklist for the initial application

1. Find a lawyer who should provide you with a checklist clearly stating what the lawyer will provide and what you are expected to do and provide.
2. Make an appointment with the French Consulate (VFS Global) near you and get a copy of their checklist. It might not be the same as your lawyer's checklist.
3. Download the application form.
4. Get photos made, paying particular attention to the requirements.
5. The French government charges for visa: $ 115 application fee, and the € 250 medical exam fee
6. Estimated private medical insurance € 900.00 for first year.

Appendix II

These were the requirements on the French Consulate website the time I first applied:

"Long stay visitors visa holders will be allowed to reside in France for up to 12 months or according to the length of the visa issued and purpose of stay. Long stay visa holders will have to register to the French Office of Immigration and Integration (OFII) (http://www.ofii.fr/) during the first three months of their stay.

During the validity of their visa, holders of a long stay visa are authorized to travel within the other Schengen States without a Schengen visa (for a maximum of 90 days within a six-month period).

The visitors visa allows you to enter France and stay for more than 90 days. You need a long stay visitors visa if you have sufficient personal income to stay in France WITHOUT WORKING (i.e. retirement).

PROCESSING TIME

Please, apply in advance. Do not wait for the last minute. You may apply no earlier than 3 months before your departure date. Processing takes about 14 days. Please apply in advance, do not wait until the last minute.

IMPORTANT: Due to the higher number of applicants during the months of JUNE, JULY, AUGUST and DECEMBER, we strongly suggest to apply at least 3 weeks before your departure or earlier in order to avoid delays. No emergency visas will be issued.

APPLICATION REQUIREMENTS

You must provide the ORIGINAL documents + 1 PHOTOCOPY of each document submitted with the application.

One passport = one set of visa documents (i.e. a family of 4 visa applicants = 4 sets of visa documents = 4 appointments)

We insist that you take the utmost care of presenting a complete visa application on the day of your appointment. Our office is not responsible for delays or missed flights due to incomplete or last minute visa application.

PROOF OF RESIDENCY IN OUR CONSULATE'S JURISDICTION

The French Consulate in Los Angeles only accepts applicants who are residents from: Arizona, Colorado, New Mexico, Southern California, and Southern Nevada.

You will have to show us at least ONE of the following documents: a valid driver license or state ID from one of these states, which must be located in the consulate's jurisdiction or a valid student ID from a university located in one of these states (or a statement issued within the past 2 months from the registrar of your university, which must be located in the consulate's jurisdiction) or an original lease or rental agreement in the applicant's name or a house deed plus a recent utility bill in the applicant's name with an address located in the consulate's jurisdiction.

ORIGINAL PASSPORT

Original **passport (+ ONE COPY** of the identity and relevant pages) Must be valid for at least **three months after your return to the U.S.**

Has least **two blank pages** left to affix the visa (amendment pages are not suitable for visas).

Has been delivered **less than 10 years ago** date of first issuance (i.e. your passport *CANNOT* be older than 10 years)

Be in good condition (i.e. not torn or damaged)

If you are not a US citizen: Proof of legal residency in the United States: A valid U.S. permanent residence card ("green card") **+ ONE COPY** *Refugee travel documents and US Re-entry permits are not accepted.*

PROCESSING FEE

Processing fee for a long stay visa is to be paid in person on the day of the appointment.

(Visa/MasterCard ONLY, preferably debit card).

APPLICATION FORM

One long stay visa **APPLICATION FORM** filled out completely and signed by the applicant. Please remember to indicate a date of departure from the US to France on question number 26 as well as the number of months you wish to stay in France.

PASSPORT PHOTO

ONE PASSPORT PHOTO. Do not glue or staple. 2x2". No older than 6 months, in color, on a plain white background, on photo quality paper, your face must fill about 75-80% of the photograph, no glasses, no smiling, taken facing the camera, no side or angled view, uncovered except for religious reasons.

LONG STAY or TEMPORARY STAY FORM

Please fill out this form and check the box indicating whether you want to apply for a long stay visitor visa "long stay" or "temporary stay".

OFII RESIDENCY FORM

One **OFII RESIDENCE FORM** duly filled out (upper part only) by applicants who will be staying in France for more than 12 months (allowing an extension at the Préfecture during the last 2 months of the visa) **(+ ONE COPY)**

For further information on the OFII procedure and processing fees to be completed in France, please check the residence permit page.

STATEMENT OF PURPOSE

A letter signed by the applicant describing the purpose of stay in France indicating your dates of stay in France.
If you are currently employed you must provide proof that you are on sabbatical such as an official letter from your employer or a notarized statement that you plan to cease employment.

SIGNED LETTER PROMISING NOT TO ENGAGE IN ANY PAID OR COMMERCIAL ACTIVITY WHILE IN FRANCE

Please make sure to indicate your dates of stay in France in the statement.

PROOF OF FINANCIAL MEANS

Provide your last 2 monthly personal bank statements from the U.S. checking and/or savings only showing monthly balance and your name. *Please print all pages of the monthly statement.* (No investments, no stocks/bonds, include only liquid funds. 401k/IRA or retirement funds are accepted only if you are officially retired) Bank statements should show that you have enough money for the entire duration of your stay **(+ ONE COPY)**

PROOF OF TRAVEL INSURANCE

A confirmation/certificate of coverage of your travel insurance (minimum coverage $50,000) without any deductible during your whole stay in France (must indicate "valid
outside of the USA or "valid worldwide" and indicate starting date and ending date)

PROOF OF ACCOMMODATION

If you are the owner of the property: 1) title deeds 2) recent "taxes foncières" 3) recent utility bill with name and address.

If you are renting the property: official lease/rental contract signed by both parties.

If you are hosted: If the host is the owner of the property: 1) original invitation letter indicating exact dates of stay 2) recent "taxes foncières" 3) recent utility bill with name and address 4) copy of host's valid French ID or residency permit .

If the host is renting the property: original invitation letter indicating exact dates of stay 2) official lease/rental contract signed by both parties 3) recent utility bill with name and address 4) copy of host's valid French ID or residency permit (+ ONE COPY of each document)

FOR ACCOMPANYING SPOUSE

In addition to all the documents listed above, please provide: Marriage license (+ ONE COPY).

A SELF-ADDRESSED FEDEX AIRBILL AND ENVELOPE

To mail back your passport, please provide a self-addressed FedEx Express "US Airbill" or an online prepaid FedEx Airbill and FedEx envelope (one envelope per family - up to 6 passports)   for US Airbill, please fill out your own address twice (you are the sender AND the recipient).

DO NOT write the address of the consulate on the airbill.

We will NOT accept other methods of delivery: NO USPS, NO UPS, NO FedEx Ground service.

IMPORTANT INFORMATION

The consular administration has full authority to evaluate and request more documents than those submitted by the applicant. Please be aware that submitting the aforementioned documents does not guarantee the approval of the visa. The French Consulate in Los Angeles can refuse the issuance of a visa.

MAKE AN APPOINTMENT

Every applicant must apply in person and must make an appointment on our website. No exceptions. Fingerprints and a photograph must be taken in our premises in Los Angeles.

Children under the age of 6 are not required to be present if applying for a LONG STAY visa, however an appointment has to be booked under their name.

If you are not able to attend, please free a slot by canceling or rescheduling your appointment by logging back in the appointment system and click on "changing your appointment." You will need your "LAX" confirmation number and passport number.

One appointment = one person (for instance, family of four must take four appointments) Due to the high number of applicants, the French Consulate reserves the right to cancel appointments made by the same person on the same day (or even on two different dates).

Appendix III

Visa Renewal Checklist

1. Appointment for renewal must apply online within 6 months of end of visa (no sooner)
2. Copy of visa from passport
3. Copy of official passport page with photo
4. Actual passport TAKE WITH YOU
5. 3 recent identity photos, size 3.5 x 4.5 cm – there are photo booths at train stations and Metro stations
6. Rent receipts
7. Lease
8. Poof of medical insurance (Carte Vitale)
9. Proof of income Social Security letter by official translator about €50.
10. Birth certificate official translation also about €50
11. Signed copy of immigration physical report
12. Bank statements – I took both my New York bank statements in English as well as my French bank statements. (You must have a French bank account to renew).
13. Letter of desire for staying in France
14. Letter from doctor – stating you are under this doctor's care
15. Statement that I won't seek employment (took in my original letter but they had a form letter to sign)
16. You'll have to fill out a form when you arrive. This flustered me, but luckily I'd brought all the information they needed. I suggest you go in a few days before your appointment and pick up a blank form. (I brought a copy of my completed original form)
17. Then you wait for a text message telling you went to pick up your new visa.
18. Renewal Fee € 269. (Bring receipt of tax paid online)

19. You must have a French phone number because they will notify via text message of your appointment to pick up your new via. They will not accept a foreign number.

Appendix IV

On the following page is a copy in English of the two-page visa application. While it may have changed, I doubt the information they require has changed. Use it as a guideline.

Liberté • Égalité • Fraternité
RÉPUBLIQUE FRANÇAISE

FRENCH REPUBLIC

LONG-STAY VISA APPLICATION FORM
This application form is free

IDENTITY
PHOTOGRAPH

EMBASSY OR CONSULATE STAMP	BOX FOR VISA NUMBER STICKER

1. Surname (Family name)	**For official use only**
2. Former surname(s)	Application date:
3. First name(s)	

4. Date of birth (day-month-year)	5. Place of birth	7. Current nationality	Application number:
	6. Country of birth	Nationality at birth, if different:	
			Processing officer(s):

8. Sex ☐ Male ☐ Female

9. Marital status ☐ Single ☐ Married ☐ Separated ☐ Divorced ☐ Widow(er)
☐ Other (please specify)

Marginal entries

10. For minors: Surname, first name, address (if different from applicant's) and nationality of parental authority / legal guardian

11. National identity number, where applicable:

12. Type of travel document
☐ Diplomatic passport   ☐ Service passport
☐ Official passport   ☐ Special passport
☐ Ordinary passport   ☐ Other travel document (please specify):

13. Number of travel document	14. Date of issue (DD/MM/YY)	15. Valid until (DD/MM/YY)	16. Issued by

17. Applicant's home address (no., street, city, postcode, country)

18. Email address	19. Telephone number(s)

20. If you are resident in a country other than the country of current nationality, please state:

Number of residence permit	Date of issue	Valid until

21. Current occupation

22. Employer (employer's address, email and telephone number) - For students, name and address of educational institution

OFFICIAL DECISION

Date:

23. I request a visa for the following purpose:
☐ Employment   ☐ Studies   ☐ Training period/education   ☐ Marriage   ☐ Medical reasons
☐ Family stay   ☐ Private stay/Visitor   ☐ Re-entry visa
☐ Official taking up of duties ☐ Other (please specify): ....

☐ GRANTED
☐ REFUSED

24. Name, address, email address and telephone number in France of inviting employer / host institution / family member, etc.

25. What will be your address in France during your stay?

26. Intended date of entry into France or the Schengen Area

27. Intended duration of stay on the territory of France

☐ Between 3 and 6 months ☐ From 6 months to one year ☐ More than one year

28. If you intend to stay in France with members of your family, please state:

Family relationship	Surname(s), first name(s)	Date of birth (DD/MM/YY)	Nationality

29. What will be your means of support in France?

Will you be granted a scholarship? ☐ YES ☐ NO

If yes, write the name, address, email address and telephone number of the institution and the amount of the scholarship:

30. Will you be supported by one or several person(s) in France? ☐ YES ☐ NO

If yes, state their name, nationality, occupation, email address and telephone number:

31. Are members of your family resident in France? ☐ YES ☐ NO

If yes, state their name, nationality, relationship with you, address, email address and telephone number:

32. Have you been resident in France for more than three consecutive months? ☐ YES ☐ NO

If yes, specify at which date(s) and for what purpose

At which address(es)?

I am aware of and consent to the following: the collection of the data required by this application form and the taking of my photograph and, if applicable, the taking of fingerprints, are mandatory for the examination of the visa application; and any personal data concerning me which appear on the visa application form, as well as my fingerprints and my photograph will be supplied to the relevant French authorities and processed by those authorities, for the purposes of a decision on my visa application.

Such data as well as data concerning the decision taken on my application or a decision whether to annul or revoke a visa issued will be entered into, and stored in the French VISABIO biometric database for a maximum period of five years, during which it will be accessible to the visa authorities and the authorities competent for carrying out checks on visas at borders, national immigration and asylum authorities for the purposes of verifying whether the conditions for the legal entry into, stay and residence on the territory of France are fulfilled, and of identifying persons who do not or who no longer fulfil these conditions. Under certain conditions the data will also be available to designated French authorities and to Europol for the purpose of the prevention, detection and investigation of terrorist offences and of other serious criminal offences. The French authority responsible for processing the data is: [...].

Pursuant to Act No 78-17 of 6 January 1978 on Data Processing, Files and Individual Liberties, I am aware that I have the right to obtain from the French government the communication of the data relating to me recorded in the VISABIO database and the right to request that such data which are inaccurate be corrected or possibly deleted only if processed unlawfully. This right of access to and possible correction of such data shall be exercised by applying to the head of mission or consular post. It may be possible to refer to the National Commission on Data Processing and Liberties (CNIL) if I choose to question the conditions under which the personal data relating to me are protected.

I am aware that any incomplete application will increase the risk of my visa application being refused by the consular authority and that the said authority may have to retain my passport while my application is being processed.

I declare that to the best of my knowledge all particulars supplied by me are correct and complete. I am aware that any false statements will lead to my application being rejected or to the annulment of a visa already granted and may also render me liable to prosecution under French law.

I undertake to leave the French territory before the expiry of the visa, if granted, and if I have been refused the right to stay in France after the expiry of the visa.

Place and date	Signature (for minors, signature of the parental authority / legal guardian)

Dear Reader, Thank you for choosing this book from among the millions available on Amazon. The author would greatly appreciate you posting a review on Amazon. For additional comments and questions he can be reached directly at:

douglaswarrenauthor@gmail.com

More books by Douglas Warren available on Amazon:

Nefarious Pleasures

Nefarious by Nature

Different Worlds

Kate

The Pink Poodle and Other Stories

Montmartre Stairs: A Paris Love Story

Hôtel Inspire

The Trickster

Made in United States
Troutdale, OR
11/07/2024

24523866R10027